Plus

EXtreme Animals

The Creepiest Animals

by Connie Colwell Miller

Consulting Editor: Gail Saunders-Smith, PhD

Consultant: Tanya Dewey, PhD
University of Michigan Museum of Zoology

CAPSTONE PRESS
a capstone imprint

Pebble Plus is published by Capstone Press,
151 Good Counsel Drive, P.O. Box 669, Mankato, Minnesota 56002.
www.capstonepub.com

 Books published by Capstone Press are manufactured with paper
containing at least 10 percent post-consumer waste.

Library of Congress Cataloging-in-Publication Data
Miller, Connie Colwell, 1976–
   The creepiest animals / by Connie Colwell Miller.
      p. cm. — (Pebble plus. Extreme animals)
   Includes bibliographical references and index.
   Summary: "Simple text and photographs present the world's creepiest animals"—Provided by publisher.
   ISBN 978-1-4296-5308-4 (library binding)
   ISBN 978-1-4296-6207-9 (paperback)
   1. Animals—Juvenile literature. I. Title. II. Series.
QL49.M619 2011
590—dc22   2010028752

Editorial Credits

Katy Kudela, editor; Heidi Thompson, designer; Marcie Spence, media researcher; Laura Manthe, production specialist

Photo Credits

Frans Lanting/www.lanting.com: 13; Getty Images, Inc.: Michael Nagle, 7; Minden Pictures: David Shale, 15; Nature
Picture Library: Jim Clare, 21; Nico Smit, University of Johannesburg, South Africa, 17; Shutterstock: JD, 5, ncn18,
cover, photobar, 1, Shane Wilson Link, 19, Smit, 11, Turi Tamas; Visuals Unlimited: Ken Catania, 9

Note to Parents and Teachers

The Extreme Animals series supports national science standards related to life science.
This book describes and illustrates creepy animals. The images support early readers in
understanding the text. The repetition of words and phrases helps early readers learn new
words. This book also introduces early readers to subject-specific vocabulary words, which are
defined in the Glossary section. Early readers may need assistance to read some words and to
use the Table of Contents, Glossary, Read More, Internet Sites, and Index sections of the book.

Printed in the United States of America in North Mankato, Minnesota.
092010   005933CGS11

Table of Contents

Creepy. 4

Creepier 10

Creepiest 16

Glossary 22

Read More 23

Internet Sites. 23

Index 24

Creepy

They are hairy! They are wrinkly!

They have razor-sharp teeth!

These animals aren't just creepy.

Their creepiness is EXTREME.

A crocodile lurks in the water.

Its eyes peek above the surface.

Snap! The crocodile's sharp teeth

catch a meal.

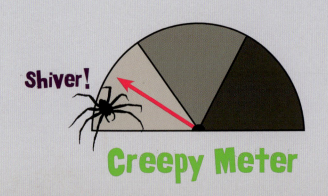

Shiver!

Creepy Meter

A wrinkly Sphynx

has almost no hair.

An owner must wipe the oils off

the cat's skin to keep it clean.

How does a star-nosed mole

find food? This mole has

22 tentacles on its face.

These fleshy feelers

help a mole find food.

Creepier

Cockroaches crowd inside homes. These creepy pests are hard to kill. They can live for more than a week without their heads.

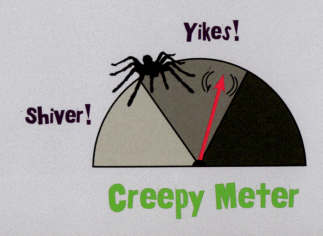

Yikes!

Shiver!

Creepy Meter

Sitting high in a tree,

an aye-aye looks for food.

Its ratlike teeth dig into bark.

Its long middle fingers

scoop out squirmy larvae.

An anglerfish swims in the sea.

It wiggles the spine on its snout

to lure fish to its mouth.

Chomp! An anglerfish

catches its prey.

Creepiest

The tongue-eating louse is

a super-creepy parasite.

It attaches itself to

the tongues of fish.

It sucks out blood. Eww!

Yikes!

Shiver!

AHHH!

Creepy Meter

Some tarantulas grow
as big as a dinner plate!
This spider looks scary.
But its bite is less dangerous
to people than a bee sting.

In the dark of night,

a vampire bat sneaks up

on its prey. Munch!

This hungry bat licks up blood

with its tongue.

Glossary

extreme—very great

larva—an insect at the stage of development between an egg and a pupa; larvae look like worms

lure—to attract and perhaps lead someone or some creature into a trap

parasite—an animal or plant that gets its food by living on or inside another animal or plant

prey—an animal that is hunted by another animal for food

snout—the long front part of an animal's head

tentacle—a long flexible structure usually around the head or mouth of an animal; tentacles are used for moving, feeling, and grasping

Read More

Seymour, Simon. *Creepy Creatures.* See in 3-D. New York: Scholastic Inc., 2006.

Stout, Frankie. *Nature's Nastiest Biters.* Extreme Animals. New York: PowerKids Press, 2008.

Internet Sites

FactHound offers a safe, fun way to find Internet sites related to this book. All of the sites on FactHound have been researched by our staff.

Here's all you do:

Visit *www.facthound.com*

Type in this code: 9781429653084

Super-cool stuff! Check out projects, games and lots more at **www.capstonekids.com**

Index

aye-ayes, 12

blood, 16, 20

cats, 6

cockroaches, 10

crocodiles, 4

fish, 14, 16

larvae, 12

moles, 8

parasites, 16

tarantulas, 18

teeth, 4, 12

vampire bats, 20

Word Count: 222
Grade: 1
Early-Intervention Level: 19